CASTLE OF DREAMS

CASTLE OF
DREAMS

DORIS LOUISE RANNOW BREN

FOR MY CHILDREN,
GRANDCHILDREN,
GREAT GRANDCHILDREN
AND THE CHILDREN YET TO COME

CONTENTS

PART I — ANOTHER TIME

PART II — ANOTHER PLACE

PART III — ANOTHER DAY

ILLUSTRATIONS

PART I – ANOTHER TIME

I REMEMBER GRANDMA

There were horses and buggies, wagons and sleds, open porches with fancy posts, large wooden clothes racks, and washing machines of wood. Grandma washed her clothes outside in summer. She had a wooden washer with a crank you operated by hand and also a hand-cranked wringer. She scrubbed and scrubbed on a huge old wash-board. She wore long dresses and big flappy aprons, always with pockets. She made her own aprons and had dresses made for her. She used all the leftover material to make piece-quilts. She had a treadle sewing machine but sometimes sewed the cut pieces all together by hand. As she stitched each block, she used a threaded needle to keep all the blocks in one neat pile.

She read a lot in the Bible, mostly aloud to Grandpa because his eyesight was so poor, he could not read for himself. All the newspapers, church papers, letters, and such were read aloud to him, some in German. She carried in her own wood to her parlor wood stove and piled it neatly on newspaper on the floor.

She always had peppermints and lemon drops in her dresser drawers. If we asked her for candy, she would give us each one piece and told us to "suck it. It will last longer." There were times we got either rock candy or horehound sticks. I could "take" the rock candy, hard as it was, but found the horehound candy very displeasing.

WHEN WE PLANNED A TRIP YEARS AGO, it was in a Model T Ford. My cousins, Uncle, and Aunt usually went too. They also had a Model T Ford car. One fall in 1926, our two families planned a long trip to the Mille Lacs Lake resort area. We did not have trunks to carry suitcases or top carriers. Ours was a folding rack carrier that fastened to the running board of a car. Grandma always waited outside of a car until it was started and running smoothly. I never knew why, but I guessed she was afraid it might blow up or something. Anyway, after it was running, we all piled in, and I do mean "piled in." There was no car seat room for me at all. I ended up seated on a little red chair between Grandpa and Grandma's feet! This is how I rode for my small years. This was going to be a long dusty trip. We traveled slowly, and roads were all or mostly gravel. My father usually had the "lead car," with Uncle, Aunt, and cousins following close behind. We kept a very close watch to see that my uncle was keeping up. Many times we stopped, waiting until they were in sight once more. Often it meant a trip back to find them fixing a flat tire or some engine problem. On one of these stops, Grandma decided to ride with them awhile, so we changed a few seat places and went on our way again. Very soon we found their car not in sight again, so back we went, to find they were all out of the car, putting out a fire under the front seat. Of course, Grandma came back with us again.

We finally arrived at our cabin near the big lake. We didn't know it then, but here began another stretch of problems. First, there weren't enough beds to sleep in. "Well," Grandpa said, "I will sleep on the floor."

So some of the men did sleep on the floor. I don't remember a lot of that night except we, the mamas, and Grandma slept cross-wise on what few beds there were.

It didn't take long, that many noises filled the night. Besides the owls and creatures of the night, my Mama heard some queer rattling noise and suspected somebody was out there trying to take off with our cars. Grandpa was first to get up and ready to go see what the commotion was. Well, it was a very windy night, and a loose old pump handle in a terrific wind can make an awful lot of rattling noises. After that episode, the rest of the night was spent in peaceful sleep.

Early in the morning, Mama decided to take pictures. So my cousin and I faithfully posed on the sunny side of the cottage. He was wearing a blue and white sailor suit. I wore a tan pongee dress that my Mama made. My little sister will not pose with us. She was about two years old, but for reasons of her own, she seldom ever wanted a picture taken.

The men in the group had wished very strongly to go out on the lake, fishing. The wind continued to blow hard, and waves on the water were very high. The women did not want anyone to go out in a boat. I am sure they tried very hard. Another thing I remember is where we stopped to watch deer in a park. It was enclosed with a high wire fence and was at the side of a road. Most of the scenery appeared very flat and very dusty to me.

In September of 1927, my cousin and I began first grade. I would be six in October, and he was six in May. As we lived on farms only steps apart, we became close friends. I was afraid when it came to school, and my fear came out as totally "not speaking" to the teacher. I held up strong on this for about two weeks. Recesses were fun, but class was not. Because I would not count the tiny colored sticks, this teacher had me sit in one corner facing the wall. In my hands were held all those little sticks. The teacher said, "When you count them, you may leave that corner." When noontime came, my other cousin came for me to eat my dinner pail lunch with her. She was about twelve then and sort of took to watching over her young brother and me. The teacher let me go for my lunch. I began talking soon after this and discovered school to be a lot of fun and, from then on, did not want to miss a single day of it.

We also made trips to Bertha, Minnesota, to visit relatives. It always meant days of planning. Roads were poor and had to be traveled in summer or fall and not at night. These trips were interesting and amusing and great fun to get ready for. Traveling usually was in the same manner, with our car in front and Uncle's behind. We stopped in town on the way one time, and Grandma bought my favorite, those delicious huge raised and sugared doughnuts. I begged to have one right away, but Grandma was stern. "No; wait 'til we stop to eat," she said.

We rode on a long way farther, finally stopping at the roadside. They didn't have so many parks and places to eat like now. I was so anxious for one of those doughnuts; can you imagine my horror when those lovely doughnuts were all heavily coated not with sugar and sweet, but with salt and awful! We could not return them, as we were many miles from that town. So the doughnuts were dumped by the roadside. Oh, how disappointed I was! I always wondered if any animal ever ate them.

There was a small farmstead between our farm and our uncle's. The family had one son living there, and this couple spent a lot of time fighting. When things got real bad, she would come over, crying and barefoot, to our house. Her dresses were always torn and dirty. We all called her "Tanta Bata." I don't think I ever knew her real name. Grandma always asked her to come in to sit and have coffee while they talked. Grandma never failed to listen to her troubles, got her to stop crying, and gave her eggs or something else to take home with her. They had little food or money, clothes, or anything else.

If a hobo off the roads stopped at our door, Grandma fed him, but he could not enter the house. He was to sit outside on the walk, and she brought food and drink out to him. Believe me, they did as she asked, and she was not afraid of anyone. She was a remarkable person. Grandma got me to do chores even when I didn't want to.

We had cows, pigs, chickens, and ducks, plus guineas for a short time. So when butchering day came, it was exciting for kids to watch. We usually had help from our uncle too. It doesn't sound pleasant, but blood was caught for the purpose of making it into sausage. Grandma could do it best. Mixed with head cheese and served with syrup over all was a delicacy I shall not forget. It is not made the same today, nor does it taste like then. Sausages were made to be smoked in our own smoke house. Grandpa was official fire keeper. The canning of meat was a long tedious job, as we had no freezer, so meat was all cut and canned. Some roasts were frozen outdoors and stored for a short while in wash tubs to be used fast.

We had an exciting evening one stormy night when I was six years old. My parents were having a night out, and Grandma and Grandpa were our sitters. My sister and I were lying on our parents' bed, watching the lightning. We saw a bright fire; someone's barn had caught fire. Next we heard a loud crash from the barn. Grandpa went to investigate. It seems a couple horses were fighting, and one had kicked and busted a tall partition. This wasn't enough for one night. Our phone rang, and Grandma answered. The next-door neighbor was afraid. Grandma Perkins was at home alone, and one of their Mexican laborers was "hoopin' and hollerin'" around her house, trying to break in. He liked his liquor too much. She wanted Grandpa to come over and protect her. Well, you may bet your last nickel, Grandma never let Grandpa out of our house again that night. I heard no more about Grandma Perkins' fright. This seemed to be such a frightful evening. I expect Grandpa and Grandma remembered it a long time.

We liked homemade food because that is what we usually had. We looked forward to homemade ice cream but had to have the ice first. There were always too many "lickers" for the dasher also, as it seemed that the ice cream on the dasher tasted better than the dished out portions.

Our mail box was quite a distance from our door, so it meant a walk to get it. Grandpa had us wait until he knew the mailman had been there; then we would walk down the gravel road, holding Grandpa's hand. He would let us carry some back too.

Grandpa's eyesight became very poor, and he always used a cane. He smoked a pipe and loved to sit outdoors in summer on an old leather seat removed from an old car. We played a lot around him, clambering over the seat, but it did annoy him sometimes, even though he never said so. He would just get up and go inside the house.

We also had a duck coop built of old house shutters. It had all those moveable slats. We made a lot of mud pies. When this coop wasn't available, we used the corn crib. It was a big job getting all those dolls, dishes, and things out there – what fun! Except when bees came in. Then we went out. It was terrible when we were told to move all our dolls out, as the crib was needed for corn again.

Winter meant sled rides and snowmen. Getting to school on time was hard. We had to be taken by sled and horses when the cars wouldn't start or if the snow was too deep, and when it wasn't real cold, we had to walk. We were so bundled up by our mamas, only our eyes were left uncovered. They would wind scarves around and around our heads and over our noses. I think my scarf was ten feet long. My fingers got cold but not my head. We didn't have snow pants, but we had long union suits with flap openings. What an ugly sight we were in that underwear. I could never get the underwear neat enough so it wouldn't show through the long stockings. Winter-wear lasted too long to suit me. Waiting for summer seemed forever!

TRIPS TO MINNEAPOLIS were "great expeditions" because they also meant a lot of preparation and planning. This trip was a visit to an uncle who lived and worked in the big city. For me, the trip was taken, again, on the little red chair. Grandma always had a lot to take along — eggs, chickens (live, of course), and all kinds of food. We had to get an early start, as it was a long way to go. The roads were still all gravel, and the hills were steep. Going down was just as scary as going up. Grandma always wanted to get out of the car and would walk up to the top of the hill or down to the bottom, whichever way we were going. Then we would pick her up again. She must have had a real fear of automobiles that never left her. We never drove to the city in winter, only in summer. The cars barely made those hills, chugging a lot to reach the top.

Our cousins in the city were twin girls who played piano and liked to sing. They had a lot of photos to look at and postcards and the good old Uncle Wiggly game. I never tired of it. Also there was a canary that sang so much, that Aunt covered the cage when we were there, as we couldn't hear each other speak. Aunt always served "holey" cheese, which I liked, and meatloaf plus other goodies. Their water always tasted funny to me. My uncle was a real sportsman who liked to fish. He also liked to lift you up and spin you around until you got dizzy. Sometimes we went walking to nearby Powderhorn Park to use the swings and teeters.

My farm cousin had a talent I envied. He could build toys, such as wagons and threshing machines that worked with belts made of twine. His wagons turned too. I tried to make some also, but mine fell apart, and Papa wasn't too happy about my using the tools and nails.

I had a very weak ankle, meaning I sprained it many times. The very first time was at my Aunt Erna's house. There was a birthday party, and we were running outside on the lawn. I slipped and fell on the grass, and my ankle hurt so bad, I cried. It was swollen, so my foot was placed in hot water and then wrapped in Grandpa's woolen sock. I'd hobble around that way awhile until the next time. One time my ankle got sprained when I was at school. I had permission to go to the store and was skipping so happily along when "bing," my ankle twisted, and there I was, sitting down on the ground. By then I always knew what had happened and also knew how painful it would be to walk the rest of that day. When school let out, we all had to walk home. It was a very long and painful walk for me.

SOME THINGS AND SOME PEOPLE greatly worried me when I was very young. I was always a bit scared of the older boys, especially the ones who liked teasing any and all girls. One day an older boy told my cousin he was going to kiss me on the way home from school. He worked on a farm after school hours and had to walk about half of the way with us. Well, I was a worried child all day in school, and when we were let out, I raced around getting out of the building as fast as I could, not waiting for any of my cousins. I bolted out the door and down the road. I ran and ran and ran and never looked back. The others were very upset with me, but I didn't care, except I was never so tuckered out in my whole life!

My parents probably never understood why I did this. I was not even happy about attending school the next day either. The boy did not threaten me again. I think, perhaps, he was afraid of being reported to his teacher. Anyway, my cousins were very peeved at me that I didn't wait so we could all walk together, as we were told to by our parents.

OUR NEIGHBORS ON ONE SIDE boarded Mexican laborers for the summer harvest season. They worked in the sugar beet fields for several years. One girl was a special friend of mine. Her two brothers did not like school and went only if they felt like it. Also they could not speak English like she could. Carmen and I became very good friends. I invited her to my home and gave her a bag of apples to take home. She must have told her parents where our apples were kept because that very evening, we were all awakened by our dogs barking. When Papa put the light on, we could see her relatives very busily putting apples into sacks to take home with them. Knowing how they were, no one went out to chase them away, but we did tell the neighbor about them. We had plenty of apples left to put away. After that, we didn't leave any apples in piles out in the orchard. They were taken into the cellar and stored away.

Grandma cut up and sliced a lot of apples to be dried before winter. It was fun to sneak this fruit as it was drying. The dried apple slices were very tasty. They made great pies and sauce in winter. Another favorite was "mebittle" — cooked in boiling water and served with raspberry sauce. I also liked sweet gooseberry pie and ground-cherry sauce. I did not like to pick gooseberries; they had so many stickers, and they had to have the stems and flower ends picked off. Picking plums was a bit better, but climbing trees to pick apples was the best. I was a bit of Tarzan, one of my favorite comics, and I gloried in climbing the branches as high as I could. Somehow I lost my enthusiasm for climbing. I would not even think about climbing a tree anymore.

Working in the garden was not my favorite chore, but Grandma had a great deal of relentless energy, and it seemed to me she could out-hoe or out-pick anyone and never be tired. Chokecherry picking time was a lot of fun! We would all hunt around, looking for pails and containers. Even the baby, he or she, was wheeled along too. Sometimes we took the old Ford pickup truck. Papa would reach the

highest cherry branches from a ladder propped against the tree; one of the elders would hold branches down, so we kids could fill our pails too. I liked to eat some, but the chokecherry gave your mouth a dry, rough feeling. The grapes grew on the garden fence and were easy to pick.

Lots of jelly jars were filled for the winter. Some grapes were packed into crocks and became wine, which was bottled and corked later. When small, we were allowed a bit of wine with water and sugar when it was served to company.

I **GUESS IT IS NORMAL** to find a child feeling a closeness greater to one parent, and I found myself closer drawn to my father as a young girl. He seemed to indulge in my childhood whims. One day when I came home from school, my Papa had a surprise for me. It was a pedal car with wings to resemble an airplane. I thought it was the most beautiful toy I had ever seen. It was three wheeled like a tricycle and had a back rudder too. I was a sort of long-legged child because my knees bumped into those magnificent wings, and Papa had to take them off, so I could ride it. I could have cried; it really hurt to see him dismantle that beautiful pedal car. It stayed around long enough though for my brother to ride when he was about two years old.

One Christmas holds many memories for me. It was at my New Grandma's home. I can remember vividly how a small oak rocker was given to me and how I worried that it would not come along to my house, but it did. I still have the rocker although the arms have been removed.

I had a girl cousin with whom I spent many hours of play. We became very close as children. We collected celluloid dolls and sewed by hand many pieces of clothing for them. We treasured them for so many years, and I often wish I could see the dolls and the clothes again. It embarrassed me when my mother wanted to show these to relatives and friends, especially to a fifteen-year-old boy cousin, but he took it all as a big joke and said they were very nice. He was ill at that time with meningitis and died the following year when he was only sixteen. He could not walk then, and I felt sad when he died.

THIS MAY SOUND VERY SILLY, but I had one uncle who scared me to death. Whenever I knew he was coming into the house, I ran and hid, usually under my parents' bed as far as I could get. He would come and look under the bed, which scared me even more. I knew he would not harm me, but it was many years before I became accustomed to his manner, and then I was not afraid anymore. On one of his visits, I was wearing a pair of girls chambray coveralls trimmed with red bands. They looked like Dutch pants at the sides. Girls did not usually wear jeans or slacks then, and I knew he would tease me immensely, so I was "under the bed" again. This time Mama had to put a dress on me, or I was never coming out while he was there, which she did.

When I became ten years old, what a happy birthday this was. I walked in, after coming home from school, and behind the door where I'd hang my coat was a big box, and in the box was a black and white puppy! He was all *mine*, and I named him Sheppie. I was so thrilled to own a dog, but my joy was short-lived. Sheppie was hit and run over by a car only a few days later. I was never given another puppy. I felt like it was my fault he got killed. For many years, we had a huge

German shepherd "police dog." He had to be tied with a chain to a clothes-line post. If he became free, he would grab the back of people's feet. I was very frightened of this dog and would only walk near if holding Grandpa's hand. The dog bit a friend of mine when she came up to the steps by our house. Her mother was at our home, papering some walls for us, and my friend came along home from school with me. Another dog we had for sometime became a vicious cat killer. My brother had something to do with this because he liked to sic this dog after small animals. So we lost all the cats we ever had that year. We had get rid the dog too.

My brother was a little trickster. If he wanted to go to Sunday school he did, but if he didn't, he just hid out where he wouldn't be found. He didn't always win out, but the duck coop was good for one Sunday. He also liked to pull hair to get his way, but sometimes both combatants ended up bawling. His hair was long and curly.

One Sunday after Christmas, we were all sitting in a front pew in church. We heard a faint musical sound near us. The sound became louder, and Mama was looking around at us. Of course it was my brother playing on a harmonica he got for Christmas. Mama confiscated the instrument, but I could feel the entire congregation peering and snickering towards us.

DID YOU EVER watch a mama put her hair up in a pug? It can be very amusing, but keep a distance away and try not to laugh out loud! It is very maddening when things don't go right. They sure did use a lot of hair pins, and they did it over and over until the results pleased them.

Back a bit, when I was four or five, was a terrifying experience that was very painful. I was playing with toys on the floor, in a favorite place near the sewing machine where a cousin was making dresses. My mama had just removed a hot rhubarb pie from the oven. The doorway to the pantry was near the sewing machine. She was trying to take the pie into the pantry and somehow tipped it, and the hot juice ran down and around my neck. It was very hot and hurt badly. I cried a lot, and they put a lot of baking soda on right away. Then I was taken to the doctor's office. The first thing that doctor did was remove the baking soda. I can imagine my screams were heard all over the town. I was bandaged heavily, and I came home to a lot of attention. I did not receive a scar.

Flu was frequent in our house and so were stomach aches. I always wondered why turpentine was used for a stomach pain. It smelled terrible, and I'm not sure it helped any. Nor the tea that Grandma made from some weeds out back by the granary. It tasted just awful. Sometimes we were given peppermint oil, which wasn't quite so bad. Castor oil was given also when needed. Ugh.

NEW GRANDMA lived a few miles away, and it was so much fun to go there. This grandma drove a Buick with cold leather seats. I stayed nights there occasionally, and it was such fun. She always read comics to us. My mama tried to drive a car, but she kept going around like a windmill and couldn't stop the car until it ran out of gas. I guess she never tried again.

New Grandma came to our house to get me. We went to town, and she bought a present for a baby. She didn't tell me whose baby, but she gave me a dime to spend for myself. I bought a small leather purse. It was brown with a snap closing. Grandma told me we were going to a party. I was excited but was surprised to find out that the party was at my own home. When we came back, there were many ladies there, and they were all looking at baby clothes. I went outside and found out from my cousin that my mother was expecting a baby! I did not believe her and said so, but she said it was true. I was very hurt that my mother hadn't told me, and I felt so stupid that I'd had to ask. I thought it was a sneaky thing to do! I was very happy though, one day after my tenth birthday, when Papa came upstairs to tell me that I had a new little baby sister. She weighed just five pounds, so she was indeed very tiny and looked just like a doll to me. So when my aunts came to see her the first time, we decided to play a small joke on them. We put my Orphan Annie dolly in the wicker baby basket. You can imagine their faces when they looked into the basket and saw a dolly.

We named this new baby, Donna Mae. I loved that name. This was one baby I could begin to fuss over, and fuss over is just what I did. It also gave me a chance to learn many things about babies; they cry, they wet and soil diapers (a lot of them), and when I started changing them (and Mama found out that I could do it), it sort of became my job. At first it was more fun than work; later it got to be a chore lots of times.

What I really loved doing was Donna Mae's blond hair, first by waving it. Later as it grew longer, I put her hair up into "ragtime" curls that hung about her shoulders. I was so proud to be a part of my baby sister's care. Making her clothes and taking her picture were also joyful events, which I never have forgotten. It was lucky for me that she was so cooperative. She was my first "real life" doll, and after her, the other "dollies" weren't played with near so much.

The Fourth of July was a truly eventful time for us. It meant we would plan a large outing of picnicking, fishing, and maybe a parade and fire works. I was an official worm digger, as I liked that job too. Packing lunch supplies was fun also (we could not forget frying pans and butter to fry fish in). The catch was prepared at lakeside by the womenfolk. The fish always tasted better then.

There was one particular cousin who always had the biggest fire crackers, and it never failed that he brought them along on the Fourth of July. My mama was so frightened of firecrackers. He knew this, so naturally he would always try to set them off near or behind her. She knew this and tried to keep an eye on him constantly. She did not always catch him, and she really "freaked" about the noise and excitement. He brought this "live-wire" act to every event. He could pop up at the time you would least expect.

The menfolk filled the boats when they went out on the lake. We often wondered why no boats ever tipped over, but they didn't. Grandpa stayed on shore as did mamas and kids. On rare occasions, a mama and maybe a girl or two would go along for a short time. We girls and small kids usually hung our feet in the water while sitting on the docks, and we spent some time picking up small shells in the sand or building sand castles. I glued one bunch of shells to a box and painted it with water colors. Long ago the shells fell off.

ONE OF MY MARRIED COUSINS rented a farm near ours, and Grandma was going there to help at silo filling time in fall. I went along to help with the cooking.

I was not going to be a lot of help, but I could carry small pails of water for them. I was repeatedly sent to the barn where water was piped and running into a water tank. This was where I filled the small pail and returned to the house with it; also there was a fence and gate about the house. I kept looking at a flock of geese nearby. I had made several trips, and so far they did not pay me any mind. Needless to say, I was very dubious about them. Maybe I looked at them too much because once more, I was sent for yet another pail of water. Perhaps this time, the geese became thirsty too because they seemed to be edging nearer and nearer to me. All at once, I didn't like their nearness anymore, and I took off on a run for the yard gate, spilling water from the pail on the way. All those geese came full gallop after me with their big wings flipping and flapping. I was so scared, I just ran my legs as fast as I could. By the time I reached the gate, there was hardly any water left in the pail. I brought it to Grandma, and she looked at it and said, "We need more than that." I just couldn't make myself go again, and neither my cousin nor Grandma ever knew why. I just couldn't tell them I was chased by geese. They went for water themselves then. I guess they figured I was tired out! Maybe they were angry at me, but I'd had my fill of those geese out there.

IN WINTER we saw a lot of snow. We didn't have plows and snow blowers as we have now. We had shovels, and all paths were hand-shoveled. So when all roads were blocked, a team was harnessed, and it pulled a sled filled with clean straw to sit in. The cream was also hauled to the creamery on the same trip. Grandma always heated irons on the cook stove; the irons were placed near our feet to help keep us warm. Also we were covered with heavy fur robes and blankets. I didn't like the straw all over my stockings and coat. Grandma and Mama came to the sled to make sure we were well tucked in with only eyes visible. A long wool scarf was wound around and around over my face, mouth, and nose. It was hard to breath, and the scarf was almost impossible to untie by myself. Papa would have on a long, long coat with a big sheepskin collar that he pulled up around his neck, a big furry cap, and long cuffed fur mittens. Off we would go, "Giddy up." It was a real nice, soft ride, but we were so heavily bundled and bedded into the straw that we couldn't see much or look around at all. We invariably arrived late for school on many winter mornings. The school bell could be heard "ding-donging," and we'd still be sledding on our way.

There were pigeons galore in our barn, and some nights we'd go pigeon catching. Mama roasted them to eat. I liked the meat then, but today I don't think about eating any. We loved the excitement of catching them. We had to wait until dark when they roosted inside the barn. Papa would take a small flashlight, and I would wait with the gunny sack ready to put them in. Sometimes our catch was small, but usually there were enough for one apiece at mealtime.

Grandma was very observant about everything that was going on, business or otherwise. If she didn't like something, she voiced her protests and then retired to her rooms after slamming her door loudly. She'd also call to Grandpa pretty sternly until he reluctantly would rise from his favorite rocker and follow her into their parlor. He used to grumble while he was doing it though, and I expect he usually just listened and let her talk it out. Anyway, after a brief while, he would return to his rocker and pipe, and Grandma would also come out and go about her house chores as if nothing had bothered her.

I HAD ANOTHER GRANDMA who lived some miles from us. I had to invent a new name for her because I couldn't call both of them just "Grandma" now, could I? So being the eldest of all her grandchildren, I named her "New Grandma." You don't suppose the other one felt she was "Old Grandma," do you? She remained just plain Grandma as always. New Grandma was my mother's mama, so we had no trouble distinguishing between our two grandmas. New Grandma was different than Grandma. My younger cousin lived with her all the time, and I envied him to have "New Grandma" so near always.

I spent some overnight visits there with them. If it was on a Saturday, I knew it meant a bath for both of us. I didn't particularly care for this, but New Grandma accepted no "buts" about it, and we were hand-bathed before bed, right by the large floor furnace register. I was shy because he was a boy, but we'd both forget the baths when at bedtime, we'd have a great big pillow fight. It got very rough because feathers flew. We thought it was fun, fun, fun — until we heard footsteps coming up the stairs. New Grandma had heard the ruckus, and it didn't sound good. She said, "That's enough now." We knew when New Grandma meant business, and we settled down and went to sleep. I wonder if New Grandma ever found all the feathers! She always read funnies to us. She saved all the funny papers and had big stacks of them. I didn't care if they were years old; to us it was always new. New Grandma sure could read good funnies! We thrilled to adventures of the Katzenjammer Kids; Tarzan, and Flash Gordon, among my many favorites. Popeye was not a favorite for me, but sometimes Little Orphan Annie was because New Grandma gave me a Little Orphan Annie doll, which I wish I'd valued. But I played hard with my dolls. That doll had molded golden curls, large white eyes, and a stuffed body and wore a bright red dress. I was about nine when Grandma let me do some hand sewing on doll clothes she cut out for me. I still have the little black plush doll coat she cut for me and helped me sew. She made many dresses and coats for us.

It wasn't many years later that she became ill with liver cancer. She spent days in the hospital, some at home, and then was gravely ill at last. I was allowed to see her just one time in the hospital, as she'd asked to see me. She kissed and hugged me when they brought me in. I realized that day that New Grandma was not going to live much longer. I felt very sad, as I loved that New Grandma very much. I knew she had never held me so tightly before. When she died, I was thirteen years old. It was just before my fourteenth birthday, and I missed her very much. I carried a bouquet of her floral arrangements at her funeral. I still treasure a china doll she gave me, a fruit bowl, and a few other pieces.

> It seems like yesterday
> She held me to her heart
> I knew she'd said goodbye
> And did not want to part

My grandma at home tried her best to teach me many things. I guess I wasn't a very good pupil, as she said I was headstrong. She did get me to dry dishes; by that I mean she looked them over, and some had to be done over. My own sister outsmarted me and hid away when dishes started rattling in the kitchen. But I, being the elder sister, could not get out of it.

Don't think it was always bad, as it wasn't. Grandma was a very smart lady and knew we had no reason not to be helpful to her. We had no television, no radio — just time to do things. We had wonderful times, playing games, climbing trees, and pumping the player piano and singing along. Papa belonged to the church choir. He was a tenor and practiced on our piano at home. I always wished I could read music and play like he did.

Grandma gave me a book, "Early Piety — Jesse Cary," copyright 1852, a very sad story that made me cry when I first read it. I have the book, and I treasure it and shall one day give it to a grandchild or great grandchild. I hope whoever becomes its owner will value it as much as I do. I have other old books and things I value. We had to buy school books then, and some are of great value today. Grandma also gave me dishes. Someday I hope to have enough shelves to display these treasures.

MAKING HAY

Making hay was done entirely with a team of horses. Mama drove a team to rake the hay. She was not fond of horses and was always afraid they would run away with her. (She was also scared of bumble bees.) After the hay was raked and dry enough, we would pick it up with a hay loader pulled behind the wagon. I went along, trying to help spread the hay on the wagon. I found it hard to do. I couldn't seem to move it around much. After the load of hay was brought to the yard, the team would have to be unhitched from the wagon and hooked up to the hay rope to pull up a sling of hay into the hay mow. I would run alongside of Mama while she drove the team. Then I would pick up the rope and guide it along back ready to pick up the next sling load of hay. I guess I liked lunch-time treats best.

THE STEAM ENGINE

The big steam engine came down the road, blowing a whistle that shook the trees! This meant threshing time on the farms in our neighborhood. What excitement this always was. Whenever we heard that whistle, we all ran out to watch the big machine come up the road. This huge monster would pull into our driveway and stand there in our yard all night! This meant a lot of cooking about to begin, big meals, many sandwiches, many pies, potatoes and meat, and big breakfasts. It took a lot of food, which also meant a lot of dish washing and wiping.

There was usually one runaway team during the noon hour too. Our neighbor's team was noted for taking off without warning. Grandma always went out to see how the grain was coming in. Grandpa was in charge of the grain wagon. There were the small accidents too, like a knife slipping in with a bundle (or a fork) or someone getting stuck by a fork. I remember this happening to a sixteen-year-old cousin. It hurt him really badly, and they put his hand in hot water.

We had a whole lot of people at meal time, when those men could sure talk. It got pretty loud around the big table. My sister made herself very scarce at these times and ate all by herself at a small table and chair. This was after everyone else was done eating. I never understood why she wouldn't eat at the table with the rest of us.

At noon the engine whistle would blow, which was a thrill to hear. We kids were not allowed to go around near the engine or the machine unless Mama, Papa, Grandma, or Grandpa was with us. We did go with to help carry lunches out. We served breakfast to some of the workers too. We were always sad to see the engine and thresher leave. It meant a long year before it came back again.

CORN PICKING

Fall was a pretty season with its colored leaves, apples to pick, kraut to cut, and seeds to shell. Corn was hand-picked with a team pulling a wagon with a bang-board. I was about fourteen when I started. The first day, my wrist swelled up so much that I had to stop until it was better, but I liked picking corn. It was fun to find a red ear. Papa brought in baskets of corn to save for seed. These cobs were placed on corn cob dryer racks, which were kept upstairs. In spring before planting, all this dry corn had to be shelled off the cobs. We did this in the middle of the kitchen floor with big baskets, tubs, and pails, filling them with shelled corn. There was corn all over the floor. I helped shell too, but it was hard on the hands.

HAIRCUTS AT HOME

None of us went to a town barber until about age seven or eight. Mama was our barber. She had a barber shears and a small hand-held clipper. My sister voiced her protests before the scissors neared her hair. I wasn't too thrilled about Mama's haircuts either. She pulled and pinched a lot. Mama sat us up on the table, and a lot of tears fell along with the hair. My first haircuts were so short and above my ears, sort of like the Buster Brown style with bangs. What I didn't understand was why my girl cousin's hair was longer than mine? By the time I entered school, Mama sent instructions to the town barber. Tell him to cut her hair, just so a "tip of the ears stick out." I remember one barber who nipped me with his clippers. I never went back to him without that awful feeling that "he's going to nip my neck again."

CHRISTMAS

December brings Christmas, and this meant a lot more baking. We were always told to be good, as "Santa Claus could be peeking in the window at us." I used to look out "kinda" scared that I might see him out there. Our tree usually stood in the dining room, next to the south porch door. We had little spiral wax candles that were held by metal spring candle holders. It was a hard task to make those candles stand upright. They were not lighted very often, mainly on Christmas Eve, after church services. I remember only one Christmas ever when Santa Claus came to our door. To me, he appeared so large I was frightened of him. He carried a sack and held out a doll stroller to me. I was afraid to take it from him. I did not speak to him at all. All I can remember is that after he was gone, I wheeled this doll stroller around and around the dining room table. I must have been only two or three years old. We also rode all our kiddy cars and wagons around this same route. We had the linoleum all worn off in this path. I learned years later that it was my own grandfather who was the Santa that I was so frightened by.

CATS

We had lots of cats. We children liked to claim certain cats as our own. They were named and played with like dolls. We dressed them in our doll clothes, bonnets and all. Then we wrapped them in blankets and, in buggies or a wagon, rolled them around. They had to put up with many rides and changes of clothes. Some kittens did not like this treatment and would run off, sometimes with our dolls clothes on them. This made us angry. Grandma didn't like to see us do this, so she would scold and told us we would be scratched. She would say "Scat," and away the cats went. She wasn't really fond of cats.

HATCHING EGGS

Getting ready for little chicks in spring, eggs were piling up in cases in the dining room. They were being "saved" for incubating time. There were two incubators, one in each parlor. Then began the job of turning eggs, keeping the lamps burning and water supply checked, and staying home. Someone always stayed home, as it was too risky to leave incubators unguarded for long periods. This was a long wait until the first eggs started cracking, but soon after that, several little chicks could be seen through the glass-front doors. They sure were cute and fluffy! Next the chicks were placed in a brooder house, under a brooder. Papa built the brooder house. They didn't stay soft and fluffy. They all became hens and roosters!

Sometimes there were steer barbeque days in town. We did not go often, but I remember well one time when we did. There were a lot of people, and Grandpa had two of us kids with him, so he held each of us by one hand. People were shoving and pushing on all sides. We were near a platform where a speaker was blasting away. He gave off this announcement, "Folks, we have a pickpocket amongst us. Please everybody watch your pocketbooks." Well, this was too late, for when Grandpa reached back into his pocket, his long purse of leather, with small change and our house key, was already missing. Grandma scolded poor Grandpa so. You know, I can't remember staying to eat. We had to climb in through a window. Poor Grandpa, I felt so sorry for him.

When we went to the county fair, we wanted to try all the rides. The fair had so few rides, it was easy to try them all. Well, I know for sure, I begged too hard for one ride. It was the one in which these chairs flew up and out while going round and round. It looked like so much more fun than the mild merry-go-round. Grandpa gave in, and I got a dime from him. I really got scared when it kept going higher and higher, faster and faster. I know now, I was just too young for it. It put a damper on my ride begging. I never begged a dime to ride again!

These small county fairs had their share of these so-called "girlie" shows. Grandpa liked to get near the tent or show entrance, enough to see maybe something (his eyesight wasn't too good). If Grandma thought he was getting too close, she'd pull him by the arm and steer him in other directions. She kept a very close eye on him.

SATURDAY NIGHT was town night. This is when the weekly shopping was done. I can still smell the sawdust on the butcher shop floor when we stopped for meat last. I liked to go in there, as no other store had this smell or this sawdust on the floor. Barber shops had baths too. This is where Papa went to take a bath. We kids were bathed in tubs at home. I didn't like waiting in the car. They never let us wait on the sidewalk. I enjoyed the J.C. Penney store in town. The store had those little coin cans on cables that were sent up to the cashier, and customers had to wait for their change and receipt to return. Sometimes the things wouldn't work, and the clerk would have to take things up the stairs to the cashier. I wondered why they used this system.

Is there anything else like new shoes? These were a big moment, especially if you got a pair and Sister or Brother did not. Nothing meant more than shiny patent leather shoes so new they had no creases. The first thing Mama did was coat that shiny surface with Vaseline. But no matter what she did, they always ended up with those ugly cracks across the fronts.

First, all we had were candles, lamps, and lanterns. In the kitchen near the west window was a large shiny reflector and a lamp holder. It still was not a very bright light, not very good for reading or sewing. Going outdoors in the dark of night was not done very often. Sometimes I'd go along with Mama and Papa to the barn. While they milked the cows, I would sit on this old-fashioned milk stool that Papa had made. It had a seat on the upper lever and on a lower shelf, which was where the milk pail would be set.

Grandpa and Grandma took care of the youngest while these chores were being done. If it was in summer, Grandpa would push a baby in a carriage up and down the dust driveway from the pump house to the corn crib and sometimes up the long driveway behind the barn and down to the back field. This roadway also led through the farm yard back to Uncle's farm, before a road went by on the other side. This was the only road out for them at that time.

Some years later Papa put in a Delco home lighting plant in our barn. Mama didn't want a gasoline engine washer, so we got our first electric Maytag washer and an iron. This meant starting the big motor in the barn every time clothes were washed or ironed; other times there would be no light or such dim lights that it was useless to use them at all. Grandma refused to use an electric iron, so she kept on using her own stove irons. She was afraid of getting a shock. Sometimes she let me iron her things. It meant being careful; if an iron happened to drop on the floor (and the irons did), toes could indeed be in great danger.

UNDERNEATH OUR DINING ROOM was a huge water cistern. This is what all the rain water ran into over summer. In spring when it was near empty, it had to be cleaned. I don't think Papa liked that job much because he had to go down into the cistern and clean it. We also had a large stock tank that was cleaned out regularly. As the water was drained, we went with little pails to catch the minnows as they came out. We also had a couple bullheads, which Papa would catch. After it was cleaned and refilled, the minnows and bullheads were put back in. Mama and Grandma never let us play around this cattle tank. We got scolded repeatedly, but it was such fun floating boards with stones on for people. I'm sure Papa knew how those stones got in the water tank!

I had my own wooden sled with metal runners and did a lot of sliding in the snow. I remember trying to build a plow out of my sled. It never worked well for me. There weren't many hilly spots, so we followed all the shoveled paths or else we climbed the straw pile and slid down. Grandpa did a lot of shoveling snow.

We had lots of animals. I can see still about six horses, though there were stalls for more. Their mangers were high and deep. Grandpa would hold me up to look at the horses. The deep mangers held many a mother cat and her kittens. When I was older, I carried grain and hay to the horses. We had only one colt, which died after a few days in the hot sun. The cow stalls were on the other side of the big barn. The pigs and piglets had their own yard and sheds. Grandpa would mix pig feed, "slop," in a large barrel on a two wheel cart. It was hard to push this cart without spilling some slop. We used to ride on the cart sometimes but not when slop was on it.

In the cluck coop, clucks were sitting on the duck eggs. As the little ducklings were being hatched, Grandma carried them in her big apron to a box behind the kitchen stove. They were fed water and oatmeal. Later when weather was warm, we put them in coops and fences outside. As they got older, they ran all over the place. We had guinea hens for about two years. The guinea hens were funny looking and made terrible noises.

There were some animals we didn't want, like a skunk in a trap. My brother didn't know what a skunk was until he got too close to it. When he came home, we all knew what happened. He didn't have any close friends for quite a while.

Grandma had to boil our milk every summer night. We had no means of refrigerating, and so milk was boiled, cooled, and set on the basement floor for the next day. She also made our cottage cheese. My sister loved it. It made me feel funny to see her gobbling up that stuff. She had to have butter and sugar on her bread too. Grandma liked to make potato pancakes. I never liked them either, but if she made mebittle, that was to my liking, and I requested it for my birthdays every time.

We had a cistern pump in the kitchen. This was supposed to pump up that rain water I spoke about. Well, it didn't always work, and even if primed with a little water, it balked. So if all failed, the big old leather couch had to be moved off the trap door, and Papa peered down with a flashlight to see how far down the water was. Then with a rope and pail, he would pull up water to fill the copper boiler, so Mama and Grandma could heat water for washing. We kids never got close to look down that dark hole into the water. Grandma was there to hold us back.

Grandma told me that they had some corn husking parties. If someone husked a red ear, that someone got to kiss anyone he or she chose. She also told me that she had traveled in a covered wagon from Illinois to Minnesota and had lived in a log cabin. She said she saw Indians but was never afraid. She was the only child in her family and kept herself always busy. In summer it was gardening, canning, and raising poultry. She saved seeds for each next spring planting. In winter she cut and pieced blocks for new quilts. She carried everything in her big aprons with the big pockets.

I REMEMBER many times and a Christmas service when snow-covered roads had to be traveled by horses and sleigh. It was snowing on the Christmas trip home too. The furry robes tickled our noses, as we were bundled so thoroughly.

I can hear the team's chains and the bells still jingle today, plus the creaks of the sleigh. Sometimes the snow was so deep, the poor horses fought to get through. They could not always make it, and we would have to give up and return home. The cream cans to be delivered to the creamery were on the sleigh and perhaps a case of eggs to be exchanged for groceries at the Biscay store.

Candy was a special treat, as we did not receive candy very often. The store had lots of penny candy and five cent bars. There were licorice cigars with real rings and the square "Fat Emma" bar with creamy white filling and rich chocolate. I really loved that bar. The old fashioned rock candy was not easy to eat, and for me, at least, horehound sticks were not a treat. Grandma said they were good for me, but I did not understand why.

Another event that stayed special in my mind was a local spelling bee. After my sister had arrived, and Mama couldn't go with us, Papa went along to the school spelling contest. We returned jubilant after, as I had placed with a blue ribbon in both the oral and the written tests.

My fishing introduction began early in life. As tots, we sat in the bottom of the boat and held our lines over the side. It sure was fun to have a fish on the line except when the fish dragged the line underneath the boat. Then an elder had to take over and retrieve the fish for us.

Some mornings we would get up at 3 a.m., so we could go fishing before chores. I would hurry out to dig for worms, and Papa would get the lines and tackle gear into the car. Later, after I was older and my brother was ready to go along, he went fishing with Papa. But I never forgot the many times we packed a few sandwiches and off we went. We always scaled and clean out our catches. I wasn't good at skinning bullheads, but I knew how to scale and clean the other fish. I liked to shore fish, but going on a boat has no interest for me anymore. I spent many nights rolling and rocking in my bed after a day on the water. We usually picked up terrific sunburns too.

My introduction to religion began as an infant. In the 1920s, most people affiliated with a church and went regularly, whether by foot, horse, or car and even wagon or sleigh rides.

Some things I shall never forget. Other things I'd like to forget and can't. Many times, my mind takes me back and wonders what would have happened if I had done something else or said something else. Grandma always told us, "What is going to be is going to be, no matter what we said or did." She put on her little flat black hat and her best lace trimmed dress and was ready for church. Amen.

PART II – ANOTHER PLACE

WALKING TO AND FRO

Walking to school was lots of fun
You saw so many things
Must not stop — keep on going
Before that school bell rings

In spring we tarried longer
When the flowers were in bloom
The purple crocus on the hillside
We brought to teacher's room

We searched for pussy willows
Even tho' we might be late
We hurry on, it's almost time
The school bell will not wait

We tarried when we came from school
There was a pond of water
And in the winter it was ice
We skated then upon 'er

There was a bridge of iron
That took us o'er the river
And here we dropped a million stones
To see them splash and quiver

We wonder if our parents
Ever knew the reasons why
We took so long a-comin' home
In days so far gone by

MAMA — WHY?

Where is my school book?
Why is it cold today?
Do I have to wear a sweater?
When will the rain go away?

How do you make a pancake?
Why is the sky so gray?
Where can I find my shoes?
Do you know any games to play?

Who put the stars in Heaven?
Why can't the baby talk?
When will she be bigger?
Will she learn to walk?

Why can't I hold my sister?
Where is my dolly's shoe?
Why can't I see Grandma?
I don't know what to do.

WHERE'VE YOU BEEN?

Does it make you wonder
Where all the time has gone?
And what you did is all forgotten
So where've you been so long?

I tried so hard to remember
All those days we were together
But when I tried to recall them
My mind went blank forever

It will never be the same again
My heart still cries inside
For what once was, is missing
And the time moved far and wide

GRANDMA'S BREAD

I remember Grandma
And how she made our bread
She kneaded and she punched it
Before she went to bed

Then early in the morning
She punched and let it rise
Once more before she put it
In tins of every size

Now she let it rise again
Until it's ready to bake
Grandma kept the fire hot
A-poking at the grate

Out from the oven
Came those loaves of bread
Ain't nothin' tasted better than
A slice with butter spread

IT'S TIME

Well, I ain't gonna' attend
No work shops,
Unless I've lost my mind.
This is the time of my life
To be sittin' on my behind.

I've "been" there and I've "seen" that
And I don't need curtains or stuff.
So curl up with the crosswords
Or one "good book" is just e'nuff!
And when I'm done with that
It's time to take a longer nap.

ALONE WITH MY SOUL

Sitting alone like a cat in a cage
No one to talk to — feeling strange
Wishing for a voice to hear or to speak
What's going on — how soon is it light?
The darkness is most lonely —
Too quiet, too still — when dawn
Awakes, sounds will fill.
Why is it so often that time stands still?
And things that move around me
Are far away, unstrained and quiet.
It is strange to feel, so different, never free,
Being caught in between the real and the fake.
I'm crying inside while my soul is awake.

Large is the key to the joys of the world
The lock when found is harder to hold.
Don't close the door tight, leave it ajar
The light from the outside may heal a small scar.

My writings have become scribbles
My walks have become shorter
My rests have become longer,
My hair is gray and thinner
Like my Grandma used to be.
I never dreamt that some day I
Could be a "someone" most like she

THE HAPPY GARDENERS

The Happy Gardeners
Are in seventh heaven
Planting in the dirt
Be it one o'clock or seven
Doesn't matter if it rains.
Flowers love the wet stuff
And veggies crave the sun
And the Happy, Happy Gardeners
Are never ever done

TEARS BEFORE BLESSINGS

I cry on the inside
And smile on the out
But my tears keep falling
Around and about.

It seems that after
I've cried and quieted down
An angel dried my tears
With a corner of her gown.

Something came and told me
All will be alright.
Just be patient for a while
You'll see a brighter light.

Blessings come in many ways.
Some will be so small,
If you do not look for them
Your eyes may miss them all

I WALKED

I walked in search of beauty
To write into my book,
I walked amidst the flowers
And a sparkling bubbly brook.

I tasted warmth and sunlight
Saw birds and insects too,
The animals went scurrying
As I came into view.

I walked in search of beauty
But traveled far in vain,
And hurried back to shelter
When pelted by the rain

SHUCKING OYSTERS

On Christmas day
They came in their shells,
Rough and unshucked
With "fishy" like smells.
With an anxious Granny
And her weapon in hand
She tackled the creatures
With an ambitious plan.
They looked awful gooey,
Like where do I pry.
Whoops! Get a good hold.
You twist while you try.
Aha! They opened
And what have I got?
It's four little oysters
Ready for the boiling pot.
After they're boiled
They are ready to eat.
So I gobbled them up
And they were a treat!

THERE IS NO PLACE

There is no place on earth below
That I can call my own
But He above has a place for me
That I shall call my home.

There is no place I'd rather be,
Than the one from Him alone
And there is where I'll hang my hat,
When I have reached that home.

TO A LITTLE BOY

I must go to town today
Packed his little clothes away
His shoes are small
His pants are tight
The little boy is quite a sight!

Soon he'll grow into a man
And then he'll walk where once he ran.
Then one day he will begin
To shave those whiskers off his chin.

A LULLABYE TO A LITTLE GIRL

Little Baby Dumpling's sweet and fair
With laughing eyes and curling hair
Two pink cheeks and a turned-up nose
Pretty little hands and tiny toes

Close your eyes and go to sleep
Little Baby Dumpling

Little Baby Dumpling's very sweet
With pretty little hands and tiny feet
Her hair is red, her eyes are blue
Little Baby Dumpling I love you

So close your eyes and go to sleep
Little Baby Dumpling

Little Baby Dumpling's grown up now
Couldn't hold her on my lap no-how
But her hairs still red, her eyes are blue
Big Baby Dumpling

I love you.

ONE SMALL WEE DOORWAY

I wrote a thousand words
To press into a book,
But they held only a candle
And one tiny look.

I conjured up a story
And felt my spirits rise,
But only three were inspired
They were Me, Myself, and I.

I built one small wee doorway
Through which my dreams conspired,
But they scattered while I pondered
My bewilderment was dire.

We write too many words
And some which never spark,
To encourage one small look
Or lighten up the dark.

We scan too many stories
And get no great oration,
If only three were touched
What gain this consternation.

We build so small our doorways
The smallest dreams edge through,
And the scattered worthless matter
Lies amongst the brilliant few.

I CRIED

I cried a million one sad tears
Because I thought you knew
But when you held me in your arms
You didn't say "I love you."

I cried because you did not say
What you were going to do
But when you held me in your arms
You didn't say "I love you."

I cried and thought my heart would break
In pieces two by two
But when you held me in your arms
You didn't say "I love you."

I cried and cried and cried and cried
If only you'd cried too
And when you held me in your arms
Had whispered "I love you."

LINES OF AGE

I know not where my steps
Will lead me, nor where
My thoughts may roam,
Because my path may
Carry me slowly and my
Heart shall keep me warm.

I've walked many miles
Both near and far with
Others and alone, I've
Cared for some and
Cried for others, but
Still I've come back home.

DEDICATION POEM TO
GRANDMA MOEHRING

She shall wear white roses in her hair
For the crown of love she has to share
And the Lord walks with her where she goes
He shall guide her through this land she knows.
For her heart is good and kind and true
And wither she walks, the Lord walks too.
Her eyes like sunshine brighten the day
Her smile disperses the clouds of gray.
Her love overflows to one and all
She speaks to the large and to the small,
She carries no hate within her heart
And from her love none wish to part.

ACH, MINE ACHING

Ach, mine aching heart
If I could but feel the love I choose
Where could I find such happiness
But with wine and bottles of booze.

Ach, mine aching back
If I could find a place to lie and rest
Where could I find such happiness
But with a lazy no-good pest.

Ach, mine aching mind
If I could find a love-filled book
Where could I find such happiness
But in a place I'd never look.

Ach, mine aching soul
If I could find a heaven on earth
Where could I find such a place
That none shall 'ere be worth.

Ach, mine aching hand
I've written so much trash
Where could I ever have found
These heaps of rotten mash.

FARMER

He stands there, silent, looking it over,
His fields of grain and nearby clover.
And he plods along — looking for a song
Doin' what's right and hatin' what's wrong.

It's spring that brings him near the earth.
With seeds to plant and reap its worth.
Many hours he spends a-lookin' it over —
His fields turned gold — his baled-up clover.

THAT ROCKING CHAIR

You cannot erase
The lines on her face.
For they hold many a care
For the times you left
        An aching heart
Behind in a rocking chair.

You cannot erase
Those graying locks
That mount upon her hair
For the times she worried
        When you left her
Behind in a rocking chair.

You cannot erase
Her memory of
The times when you were there
Or the times she held
        You on her lap
There in that rocking chair.

THAT HEARTBREAKING DAY

I saw you kneel at the alter
And brush a tear away.
I wanted to kneel down beside you
That heartbreaking day.

I felt the crying inside you
And saw you push it away.
Your eyes both said she had hurt you
That heartbreaking day.

Please let me pray there beside you.
Godspeed your tears away.
As we pray may we feel His comfort
This heartbreaking day.

She told us that she was leaving
And going so far away.
Our hearts were falling in pieces
That heartbreaking day.

We pray that the path she has chosen
The Lord will help lead the way
And together we'll send Him our prayers
This heartbreaking day

A WALK

We took a walk to the Land of Dreams —
So quiet, so peaceful —
The trees stood still and the grass was asleep it seems.
My footsteps barely heard on the soft wet ground
The gentlest of winds blew lazily about over the small bushes that grew around.
I silently knew my thoughts were adrift.
In this place of enchantment, no worries exist.
Oh for a world of make-believe, where no sorrow is known and in Peace we could live.

BEAUTY IN A FLOWER

Beneath the heaven of blue
Earth wills for you and me
The flowers in splendid beauty
Send forth their colors to see.

Scented as many perfumes
Painted with every hue,
Shaped like a million jewels
Each year spring up anew.

Each and every bud of flower
Has its own moment to bloom,
And while its beauty fades and dies
It leaves us all too soon.

TENDER PETALS

In a flower's tender petals
Lies a sweetness still untouched
'Til a storm of summer's roughness
Spreads down upon this earth.

In a baby's soft-skinned hand
Lies a mother's tear-filled heart
Like a blossom spreads its petals
This flower needs her start.

In a heart of truth and kindness
Lies the dreams of many past
And a future deep with flowers
Holds a love from first to last.

THE SHADES OF NIGHT

The shades of night draw closer.
I search for compassion among my memories
Reaching for summits of tenderness
Fleeting pictures one hardly sees
Passages swim before my eyes
I look for soothing phrases of thoughtfulness
For close beside me and ever near
Is a door that opens with selfishness.
Do we not put others back in mind
When trials befall our long spent day?
And do we not close our eyes to other's woe
Nor feel another's wayward way?

Lest we speak often of pride and fall
We shall feel as another who fell and rose
And held His head up high
Who passed Him hope He never knows.
But deep inside their small weak hearts
A spark arises throughout His breast.
"You have chosen your self-centered way
And failed to One who gave His best."
He tested your strength when you lay weak,
He closed the curtains by your bed
For now the shades of night have drawn -
He's closed your eyes and you are dead.

THE GRASS IN THE FENCE

I'm not a true artist in any sense,
But I couldn't go back to a bordered fence.
It held all the weeds and the grass you should mow,
And obscured the fence in the way it would grow.

It tangled, it snarled, it growled when you passed,
And still it held fast on the line —
The mower not reaching or nearing its nest.
And to the fence it said, "You are mine."

TOO BIG TO KNOW

There is so much I'd like to do
And so little time to do it
So many things and places to see
And all I do is sit!

Dishes to wash and floors to clean
Clothes to patch and iron too —
Meals to cook and fruit to can
And I feel awful blue!

Chickens to feed and eggs to pick
Got to get the milking done —
Hurry! Get the dinner on
All I do is run!

Beds to make and goods to sew
Flowers to plant and weeds to hoe
Seems I need more arms and legs
The world's too big to know!

So guess I'll stay right where I am
And keep on running so —
Wouldn't feel right just sitting down
The world's too big to know!

BEHIND LIE THE TRACKS

I remember Papa
And the coat he used to wear
When on a cold and blustery day
He drove the sled with care.

We sat in a bed of straw
And were bundled up so tight
We couldn't move a muscle
Or look to left or right.

This trip to school was something
With Papa at the reins
Those horses were excited
As the cold wind blew their manes.

Some drifts of snow were deeper
And it took a mighty heave
Behind us lie the tracks
That our sled and horses did leave.

TIME GROWS

Time grows longer and dreams do fade,
We climbed the hilltops and passed the grade.
We buried some comrades along the way,
And nighttime swiftly reaches the day.

Our steps grow smaller as when we began,
We search for peace and a refreshing span.
We hold onto memories that brightened our day
And lifetime suddenly ends in our way.

We think least of death as we struggle and toil,
Some tasks blossom and some end in spoil.
We'd little know pleasure if we never played
And never know God if we failed to pray.

THIS IS NOT THE TIME FOR SINGING

This is not the time for singing
We don't hear bells or ringing
Heavy leans the care on shoulders
Broken down by heavy boulders
This is not the time for singing

This is not the time for crying
Even though so many are dying
The few that stay are here to give
Make bright for those who live
This is not the time for crying

This is not the time for taking
What you feel you've gained by making
Your heart shall hurt and weary be
If you forsake your love and flee
This is not the time for taking

This is not the time for hurting
In revenge on one less caring
For his heart may only mean you well
His tide of thought didn't stay and tell
This is not the time for hurting

This is not the time for dying
Or to close the book while trying
Closing care and responding to none
Closing your eyes and cutting your tongue
This is not the time for dying

MAMA'S PUG

I remember Mama
With her hair in a pug.
How she pulled and yanked and twisted
And she gave a nasty tug.

How she combed and brushed and wrapped it,
And then when it was pinned,
She pulled it out and sputtered,
"I didn't like the way it leaned."

Just before she went to bed
She'd take out all the pins.
Then she brushed and combed again,
And braided whilst she spins.

Around and around her fingers
She gathered all that hair
Into one long glistening braid.
All I could do was stare.

I never ceased to marvel
At how these things were done,
Because I was a youngster
And to me, this looked like fun.

ONE DAY

One day as I was driving
I saw a girl in the town
We went for a drive in the country
And there my car broke down.

She didn't believe what I told her
I did not know what to do.
I looked beneath the car's body
And she hit me with her shoe.

She told me I was a "fresh guy"
And wanted a kiss or two.
But I was busy a-fixing my car
And off came her other shoe.

I never tried to kiss her
But that's what she wished me to do
While I was trying to tell her
She hit me with her other shoe.

So if you're a guy in the city
And spy a girl walkin' round
Don't ask to take her on a ride
Cause shoes can hammer and pound!

IT IS DONE

Winds all creaking
And moaning with pain,
Still life goes on, again and again.
   Dew drops like silver
   Shine in the sun,
Waiting 'til warmth and love have spun.

A feeling of freshness
Lingers on the air
Each day brings a newness
Never before felt there.
Seasons are waiting at earth to be blest,
Lest someone forget.

They lie unopened upon her breast,
   They heel to the wind
   They blow to the sun.
God has promised a rainbow
And to them it is done.

FORGIVE AND FORGET

Forgive and forget — is easy to say
But belief is otherwise and forget
Is a word that will not go away.

The hurt will set like poison
And rise again and again.

Sing and be happy
Play and be gay
God has helped me
To smile today!

I'll cry tomorrow
And smile today
But the hurt inside
Will not go away.

NOTHING

Like a small child, I want
Everything to be beautiful
With no pain for anyone, no hurting,
No crying, no more mistakes, love for all.
No more hate, don't cry, why?
It looks bad. Hold on, don't say it hurts.
It's inside, hurting. Where are the answers?
Hold me. Where am I? Just cry once more.
Cry no more. Please don't hurt.
Life is small. We are small.
Mama, I love you.
God, I love you.
Papa, where are you?
We are all a child forever.
How did we become what we are?
Where is the answer? I am nothing.
I was nothing.
I shall be nothing — we are all nothing.

WE CRY ALONE

We all cry alone for no one
Wants to hear our sobbing,
Our tears mean nothing
So dry up, babies, you've had it.

My heart is still crying and
My eyes are getting red,
I'm sad and very blue and
I should have stayed in bed.

The clouds are gray and cold
They make me feel much worse
If only the sun would shine today,
I would not sit here and curse!

I wanted to blame the birds and bees
But who in Hell cares about all this?
I've done to myself what I deserve
And when I die, my soul will pay.
Poor soul, run away and hide forever!
So that even one might ask "Who's so clever?"

Not him who hides from every view,
Come face the Master, He who guides
Help is needed, open your heart and cry
He who hurts, from Him he hides.

You fool yourself — you cannot hide
No matter where you go — he sees all,
Knows all, feels what you feel and
Compassion is His to give and when
You feel you've hit the bottom deck,
Pick yourself up and look above you
He is there with His open arms to
Hold you and guide your body to
High Ground.

YOU AND I

Let's sit or play a while together
And dream of happy things.
As we listen to the songs of birds
In a park with children's swings.

We could each find a swing
Or something else to do.
We could still go on dreaming
While I was pushing you.

We're never too old to dream
Or wish upon a star.
And every day we remember
How much we've done so far.

Hold those times within your heart
The days we've spent together.
Memories are what we have
To hold in our hearts forever.

MY CRIES

My cries shall go unheeded.
The floodgates have opened to Hell,
Those who wander shall perish quickly.
All who stop and hesitate to go on
Are falling fast by the sidelines.
They shall be trampled upon by foes
The enemy advances brutishly over them
Sounds of crushed bones fill the air
Stench of wretched bodies fill the soil
And soon the air is polluted with fumes.
Everywhere panic has overtaken the man
All his goals are forgotten, fear arises
The minds are fouled and tarnished,
Scrambled and poured into meaningless clumps.

Crash, the End of all things, Hell has broken loose.

REST NOW AND THEN

Be silent my heart
Don't shiver and shake
I've chosen this time
To stay wide awake.

It matters so little
What rest my soul needs
The days of my life
Need few of my deeds.

Because there just isn't
The strength of before
Once I was able
To do a lot more.

The age has moved on me
Getting older I've become
A creature of habit
To rest now and then.

KISS AND MAKE IT WELL

Run, my darling, fast away
Take your Teddy bear to play,
Hold him tightly in your arms
Bless him with your childish charms.
Graceful as a tiny deer
Hopping, skipping, falling, fear,
Just a tiny skinned-off knee,
You'll come crying back to me.
I will kiss and make it well.
You'll ne'er remember that you fell.
Hopping, skipping, falling, fear.
Just a teeny hint of tears
Falls again, a scratch perhaps.
Soothing quiet bedtime nears.

CASTLE OF DREAMS

I built a castle of dreams one day.
They all fell to earth and melted away.
And lying so silent, I watched them there
My hopes, my dreams, beyond repair.

I stared in anger, hurt and pain,
Thoughts muddled, confused inside my brain.
This is not fair, 'tis cruel, unjust.
Why must my dreams explode and bust?

My anger, slowly recoiling inside,
It found still another place to hide
And 'til I recapture my dreams as before
This castle shall never be anymore.

Those dreams were never meant to be,
All fade and disperse to eternity,
And those we capture so fleetly stay
One moment and they too pass away.

PART III – ANOTHER DAY

JANUARY 1973

It very much seems I wanted to write poetry or other stories only when I was extremely depressed or let things affect me so deeply that I had to get it out of my system in any manner or way. It was as if my hand did not even control what went onto the paper. It just sort of flowed out whether it made sense or not and made no difference if it rhymed or not. Just to write was a sort of consolation and the valve of emotions were open to flow, sometimes so fast that I could not copy quickly enough what was coming out of my head. Maybe it was because I never seemed able to spill out my thoughts or troubles to anyone. I never felt that any other person cared enough to be sympathetic to anyone else. Now I know some feel a great need to be open and shout and that there are those who can only listen; whether it be intently or absent-mindedly matters none. If you can't take anymore, you simply let it slide through, hoping each time will be the last. When it comes back again, you close your ears, and you hear only what you want to hear. Maybe it helps somehow to be able to do this. If I am meek I shall remain meek to the end of my being. Faith, perhaps I have some, but it gets harder and harder to hang onto.

Everywhere around us, spirits are breaking, compassion fails, responsibilities are almost nil, and no one wants to care too much for fear of being hurt.

Love is strange. Love is unsure. If you say you love someone, really mean it; don't hurt that someone just trying to make him feel good. Believe me, if you lie, that someone does know. The love for God must come first, then love any and all, for God is in man's image, and we must learn to trust in God and man in order to truly love. Could you truly love and care enough to give your life up so that someone you love might live?

I do not confess to being an author; the poetry is plain; the words are simple; and not everybody enjoys everything that is written. Some like Westerns; some prefer serious reading; others, true adventure; many, spicy books. I still like best the common written words, understood by all and written simply in the shortest way possible. If I can't get the meaning or reason across by simple words, I cannot write anything at all.

I can't even confess to being anything important. Sure, I can do many things, but they aren't worldly or magnificent. I am an unknown amongst many, just a small mere person hoping to keep going and fighting to come back if I get tramped on, and I do tend to let them tramp on me even if I don't like it. There have to be people like me because I just can't be one of the trampers! I shall hang back and watch the fireworks while the pushers and leaders fight among themselves. Our cares do exist but not to the point where we want to push and shove to get where we are going. We see it happen. We know we cannot help because some refuse us entry into the realm of authority. So we shuffle back behind the lines of fire and just watch quietly. When the spoils are spilled, we are the tidy ones who will step up and clean up the puddles.

Do we need to fight to be on top of everything? Why do we feel this need of authority? Why can't all people just live simple lives, wherever they might be?

Where are we going? What are we doing, and why? It is not begun by one. It is begun by many. It is carried on by many.

Can you see the mothers and daughters pick up arms and fight? Yes, we can because that is what we do. We are a mother's sons and daughters, and fighting is drilled into little heads every day — fighting is in the blood, inherited without reason. When we cease fighting anything, we are all dead. So we must let them still fight and let them all live, but each one must answer his own call and act out his own thing and take the consequences for his own actions.

What happens won't be on silver or gold platters. Who really knows what comes tomorrow or what we leave today? We may each leave some small part of us behind, but the flesh shall be obliterated, for all that is material or worldly, all just dust and ashes. The only remains are sightless, soundless space, no end, no beginning, no touch, no sense, no odor, just empty and huge dynamic space. Perhaps God shall begin all over with a new Earth, new people, everything for a new purpose. How should we know? We who are here now shall never know. It is for the best that we do not know everything. If we did, we might perhaps all turn into mentally unstable people. Our souls, if we have any, would explode in agony. We are not all-knowing and like gods, though there are those who propose to be prophets and predict our coming and going. If we are here, where are we going? If we are not here, where have we gone? If we are alive, why are we here? If we are not alive, where are we?

JULY 1975

In 1975, the last week of July, we (Jerry, Karen, Carla, Christa, and I) left for Alexandria, Virginia, on a bright, hot, and sunny Tuesday morning. I'd had a very lengthy case of summer flu just the week before and wasn't getting well very fast, so I had made up my mind to forfeit this trip. I could have cried. I felt really sad, as the trip was planned on weeks before.

The family arrived all packed and prepared to leave, and I was to accompany them. As it was, my case was not ready, having decided against going. It was only my such a very last decision, to go with. I was persuaded by Barb and the others, and they helped pack my belongings. I wasn't too sure I had everything needed, but I was sent off anyway.

I still had a nagging pain in the back of my head, which cost me loss of sleep at times, and I'd been putting heat on and taking medication from the doctor. I didn't realize my excessive thirst was a result of the medicine I was taking. If we drove past any body of water, I just felt I had to get out there and drink it all up! I felt foolish, but that's the way it was.

We arrived in Alexandria around 11 p.m. on Thursday evening. It was a joyous reunion with Jan, Ron, Eric, and Leif. We had not seen them since 1973, and those two grandsons were growing up fast!

This was our first time in Washington, D.C., a part of this country I'd never expected to see or visit. I had read in history books in elementary school about these places but never expected to ever see them. My own parents never traveled beyond the Twin Cities and Lake Itasca. And those trips were a great hassle and eventful, as I've written before in this book. The trips my parents took were traveled only in summer and with a Model T Ford car.

History was at the bottom of my list for studies, so seeing places of history was a study in itself and had to be learned all over. I discovered sort of dismally that Washington, D.C., did not exhilarate me that first night. Maybe I was too tired, partly from the effects of flu and medications. I did not feel thrilled with what I saw, but I tried hard to take it all in and enjoy it. I even wished I had taken more pictures. My heart was not entirely in focus.

Mount Vernon was very inspiring, and to see it "alive" was a thrill. The heat was incredible, and I had to get used to the high humidity the entire time, which made me treasure the visits where air conditioning was a part of the scene. I had to miss some sights. One was Ford's Theater, but time was of essence, and being not in the very best of condition for this trip, I knew we would be returning another time. Just to see Eric, Leif, Jan, and Ron again and being able to stay with them was like living at home. We hope they always feel most welcome to our home too, as our door is always open.

WE HAVE OUR SHARE OF TEARS TOO, but there are always some who have much more to bear. You will always find someone who has far worse than yourself. Many cry openly and express to others their feelings in words of disappointment and heartache. I guess there are several who would rather write into words on paper than confess their inner feelings aloud to another's ears. I well remember a day when we drove our first daughter to a college of her choice. It felt like we were taking her away from us, and in a way, it is exactly what we were doing. We cried to ourselves on the long return trip and spoke little as we both felt a sadness of separation from her.

ONE OTHER SAD, MEMORABLE DAY was when we took our first son to board an airplane trip to Texas. He had joined the Air National Guard and would be training there in camp. And he would be gone for many long months in his first long stay away from home. It did not hurt until I returned home and, at the time of our noon meal, found I began to cry and could not eat. The plane was a four engine Air Force cargo plane. It looked like a huge barn, and one engine sent out puffs of ugly black smoke. It seems as if the first one out of the nest "breaks the ice" for the rest because we take the following trips more in stride. As for now, he has been to several places on the globe, and in these times, people travel a lot more freely than when I was a small girl. We thought the sight of an airplane was a thrill to see, and we never saw a helicopter at all. Now we have space travel, which in my childhood was only in comics like Buck Rogers but ironic that one day it came to be! I still see no reason at all to live in space where there is no air to breath and no land to live on. Men never give up to new adventures no matter what or how much it costs them.

There shall always be mysteries of life; if men believed only in God, they would think He alone could know all the answers. I often wonder what this earth would have become if God's Son had never been betrayed, beaten, and buried. Would we know life as now it's known? Would we be here? I do not think so. People are human and self-interested and crave power and money. Why is there no true peace any more? What is there to be gained by the slaying of some to gain fame or fortune? How do we reconcile seeking everlasting life by committing to death our own? I have no answers, and no one can help if we see wrong and close our eyes and look the other way and if we see corruption and make believe it is not so. If we see these things, we are afraid, and in our hearts, we suffer in silence. Who are the meek among us, and where are the strong? Who will open the eyes and souls? Where will all the terror end? Only with God is everything possible.

Food today seems to taste different, perhaps from all the added preservatives and chemicals we know little about. We don't know but that these added things may be harmful in many forms. No matter what happens, there is no one to take the blame.

MARCH 3-19, 1976

Life is a confusion of ups and downs, ins and outs, hurrying one day and loafing another. Some days it is hard to begin, just as though more rest were required; the enthusiasm seemed to be lacking, also the desires. Sometimes you have to push yourself along; gladly, that is not always the problem. Other times you can awake with a great feeling of well-being, ready to take on anything and feel able to do everything.

The greatest feeling is to see a project well-finished and know you've made it the best effort you could (even if it didn't quite reach your expectations). If you love it, it is great.

Have you felt many small pains over something that just didn't turn out? Sure, it happens to all of us but that doesn't mean we give up. We just pick ourselves up and try again, just like a tot struggling to make the first steps walking. We watched five sets of feet get up and patter around our house. Mama and Papa watched five sets of feet also. Grandma and Grandpa watched six pairs of feet get started. They have all kept on climbing for many years.

Now all of the Grandpas and Grandmas have gone on to another world, one we do not know yet. We who are here must live for them as long as we can. We are a bit of their lives, so in several ways, they are still living.

In our children, we shall still be living, even though our flesh and bones are dead. It is our reward to us to see our own minds active in their accomplishments. We live through them when our lives are growing less active. It is a happy time for each new event whether it be a new birth, a new job, a graduation, or any turn in each of life's decisions.

Our minds are not as active or alert. Sometimes it hurts to stop and evaluate what might be left for us. It is much better to "ride along with the waves" and do whatever pleases us and try not to be bitter over things that depress us so much. It is natural to be unhappy over some things. I hope we do not reveal our feelings at all times. I should like to think all is well forever, but this is not possible; there will always be unpleasantness and disappointments from time to time. I pray to God that we know when to keep our mouths silent, and I pray also that we do not interfere in the lives of those loved most. There are occasions when it is hard to be still, but we know we can't live the lives of others for them or expect them to live like ours. My prayer should read like this:

God, please help me to speak wisely, but close my mouth before I
say too much. With the help of Jesus, in His name,
—Amen.

MAYBE I WRITE TOO MUCH TOO. I hope not. I've torn up pages of what I later considered trash, but it only gave me an incentive to act, even if just to prove to my own self that I can put some words down on paper. They don't seem all that important at times. I don't always copy word for word what I've written, but this is a sometime sort of diary of my life and what I could remember from my own life and whatever Grandma told me, my Papa told me, and Mama told me.

There are occasions we all fell sad and blue. Thank goodness it is not often. It is not yet my lifetime. We have all our family with us and within reach as long as they live on this earth. Papa's parents left us in 1957 and 1958. Grandma Bren was a great joy to Janis and Jerry for many years, and Mary Lou was such a joy to Grandpa Bren because she walked to him first, and he held her many times. She was only five when he died. We did not take her with to his funeral. She was told that Grandpa died in his sleep and went to heaven to be with Jesus. We had her stay with friends during the funeral. Because Barbara was not born until 1959, she never knew the kindness of Grandpa and Grandma Bren, and I have often wondered and wanted, just knowing what they would have felt, and I believe they know about her too. We know they would have loved her, and she would have loved them very much.

We do not know if we shall see great grandchildren or even all of them. We do not expect to live forever. I accept the truth that our lives on earth are just a matter of time, and I am not afraid. It is a new adventure into the unknown, just as we entered here into the unknown. We will enter adventure again.

God is good to us. He helped us make our journey, and He eases the pain that comes when we leave. We are all created as the dust of earth, and, I believe, we shall all return to dust and become extinct in time. Even what I write today will pass away. It might be around a few years, but what shall I know about that? I have this much to say — I've enjoyed the times I put thoughts down on paper. Even if this work is in any way changed, it has been my thoughts, not those of others. So let these words be, and don't pick apart into little pieces what one small mind is trying to explain.

SOME WHO HAVE PASSED on were very close. My Aunt Erna was a great lady, and Mama told me that she chose my given name, Doris, on the day of my birth in 1921. She had a marvelous way of extending love to all around her and was very kind and patient.

Grandma Emma Moehring was another great lady whom I respected very much. She lived for God and returned to Him. May Grandma Moehring's rewards in Heaven be great. (Sometimes, as here, I cannot write without tears although it has never rained tears yet without the sun returning again. We need the rain and tears to make the world clean again.)

POLITICS IS ONE THING I've never had any interest in. First, I don't understand, and what I hear is just repetition saying that the government gets whatever it wants and that people have little or nothing to say. We hear often "get rid of all those government officials and start over." Now, who could do this? And, with human nature being what it is, people would not be pleased again, and the whole thing would likely be the same all over again. I never, say never, will be a politician. However, a teacher accepts a large responsibility. If a heart is honest, a person who is a teacher will want to be the best, and if I'd lived my own life over, I would be a teacher, just an ordinary teacher, only for home economics. What kind of a teacher would I have been? We shall not know, but being a parent was sort of like being a teacher, and as parents, we begin the teaching of those in power who are building the future. When those in politics and power all pass away, our children's children, when grown, will be the next.

What few possessions we have mean little or nothing for the future. Books record the happenings, the major events, the wars, the tragedies, and everything that happens. Antiques are stored to be viewed and reviewed. What we have is not labeled or tagged, and it may be of no value whatever. I wish something better could be, but there is no one to know about these things I have. Some day I should catalog some items, and they could be placed in a small town museum. This is a wise thought; perhaps it is time to do this.

MARCH 22, 1976

I had the opportunity to see another small part of our country when Papa's brother, wife, and friend asked if I'd like to go to South Dakota and see the Black Hills. I'd only read about and seen them in pictures and books. Also we would see and go into my first underground cave and see the great Mt. Rushmore. It was during the gardening season, and I consented to go with a feeling of neglecting duties at home. But I thought if I refused, I might never see the immensely awesome sights I never dreamed of seeing. It was beautiful, and I went overboard taking slides, slides, and more slides. The famous four presidents were a sight I still treasure today. We had such a bright, sunny day with stark white clouds floating gently over the brightest blue I can remember. My slides turned out to be (I consider) my very best. We then proceeded to Mt. Rushmore cave. I never dreamt that walking and viewing the insides of the earth could be so tiring and exhausting. At first entry, it was very cool and moist; then it became very warm with surfaces wet and slippery, and passage ways were narrow and steep but entirely exalting. Even though I was happy to see daylight again, I found I have no fierce desire to explore another cave, even though all are different.

It was, and still is, a trip to be remembered and gladly recalled with all the slides and a few treasured souvenirs.

MAY 5, 1976

Yesterday was my Mother's seventy-ninth birthday. My cousins Pearl and Clara went with me to visit her and Papa. We took all the food for the dinner. Clara brought her an orchid corsage. I gave her Anchor glass salt and pepper shakers. Pearl brought a bath towel. We had such a big dinner. Clara went to shop in the Ben Franklin in Glencoe. We got home around 5 o'clock. The weather had turned much warmer, and we had a little rain last night. My four o'clocks are starting to come up and about three hills of potatoes. Pearl wants one yellow and one blue crocheted flower; the blue is for Carol.

I have finished knitting a patterned sweater for Carla. Our neighbor, Jim had a heart attack, and I want to bring him a red rose. He loves roses.

OCTOBER 10, 1980

It is hard to remember that you've had children. You brought them through babyhood, childhood, days of sickness and worry, and all those "teen" years when nothing quite satisfies and every care is multiplied a thousand-fold or more. A tiny bit of fault looms over all and seemed so important at that time. Time passes and cares grow dimmer in the mind — what once seemed too drastic is just a passing fancy. It was not a matter of life and death. Feelings of inadequacy fall far distant; the important thing is, don't worry about what others are thinking every minute; be more concerned about your own feelings towards others.

It is better to make others happy and not fill your life with thoughts or concern about yourself. Then I hurt again — deeply, inside a tearing, searing, and knotting pain. I am crying inside and overflowing with doubt. What have we done? How much hurt can we take into our heart? How much we care; we do want our children to be like ourselves. We hurt so deeply when they do not respond to our liking. The scars are never healed; the pain shall always be with us. What have we done? Where is the answer to loving and caring? How far can love hold together? I've searched into my being — but I cannot find whatever it is to heal this unknown.

I will not apologize for writing what words have been copied here in this book. I know there is probably not one person who has never in adult life had some regrets somewhere along the road. I do not admit to never having any because I did, but to protect the innocent, these things will be known only to myself and my God. We cannot go back and re-live where we went wrong — if we could, everyone would be somewhere else. We learn by failing. It is "growing up" that gives us character. Living now by days, not years, and remembering that life is really very short and even shorter as we grow older, I don't mean to be sad about what was — this all is meant to be and to be lived fully and as actively as possible.

The mind and body must both rest some time.

NOVEMBER 29, 1985

Papa's funeral was today.

It was snowing, and roads were covered with snow and ice. The funeral was well-attended in spite of the inclement weather. The casket bearers were Don and Robert Hatz, Walter Rannow, Lyle Bren, Larry Moehring, and Tom Baumann. Jan came from Falls Church, Virginia. Karen and the girls tried to make the trip, but visability was so bad that they had to turn back at Cologne and return to the Cities. It was not the best day to be on the roads.

Jan left the next morning to return by plane to Virginia. It hurts to see them leave again but we know we must.

JANUARY 1986

Mama left us on Christmas morning at 6:05 a.m., 1985. Just one month after Papa. We buried Mama later in the spring of 1986. Her funeral was on December 28, 11 a.m., at the Biscay church.

We chose a beautiful wine dress for her, and she wore the hand-laced necklace that I'd made for her many years ago. In her casket were eight tiny red roses for the great grandchildren.

It was a sunny day — not snowing, but it also was a very sad day, as now both parents are gone together. Jan came by plane again on Friday night and returned on Sunday afternoon at 5 p.m.

It is January 1986, and I should begin putting the house into order. Papers no longer to be saved must be burned. We need to get rid of items no longer in use. Why is it so hard to do this?

MAY 1987

We have been fortunate to have no unbearable tragedies happen to us. We are certainly aware of the many dangers in several areas. We are so very thankful that our family has been blessed with wonderful children, grandchildren, and, if God sends, great grandchildren some day in the future — we shall know even if we have left this crumbling old world and joined with the many who have passed on before us.

My prayers are for each one to be protected from harm and injury. If I could bear the pain and injury myself, I would not hesitate for one second even though we will not know what the future has in store for us until it happens.

Dear God of Heaven,
Keep our children all safe and warm.
Heal their scars and protect them forever.
The Lord is here forever.
We are here only for a short time.
The Lord is alive in Heaven.
We shall see the Lord.
We will not lose, we will gain.
Our hearts shall be opened.
Our eyes shall see.
The Lord is waiting.
For you and me.

Is there room at the inn?
Will He answer the door?
How soon will we know?
And where shall we be when He calls us to come?

The air is fresh.
The grass is green.
The Lord is in His Heaven.
He is watching His flock
How they work His land
How they pray for rain
How they plant the seed
How they love each other
Are we cruel and sad?
Are we doing His will?
Do we love enough?
Do we really care?

I have no answers
My mind goes blank
I only have questions
If the door does open
And He calls, will we
Know enough to answer
And will we go in?

DORIS LOUISE RANNOW BREN

I was born on October 25, 1921, at home on a farm
Daughter of George Rannow and Frieda (Jungclaus) Rannow
Attended Biscay School, McLeod County, Biscay, Minnesota
A year at Hutchinson Public School
I enjoyed sewing, needlework, drawing, and gardening
I was a child
I became a girl and a grandmother — skipped mother
I wish mother could last forever
Goodbye is never forever, however
We wait.

6735014R0

Made in the USA
Charleston, SC
01 December 2010